FREEDOM FROM POVERTY

NOTE: ALL SCRIPTURES ARE QUOTED
FROM www.biblegateway.com

TABLE OF CONTENTS

INTRODUCTION

There is a difference between the rich and the wealthy. Being rich means there's an availability of money. However, being wealthy means having the money and the systems that ensure productivity. God told Adam to be fruitful, multiply and replenish.

A wealthy person ensures the money that comes finds systems to help it multiply and increase.

Genesis 1:28

And God blessed them, and **God said unto them, Be fruitful, and multiply, and replenish the earth, and subdue it**: and have dominion over the fish of the sea, and over the fowl of the air, and over every living thing that moveth upon the earth.

God applied the same principle of establishing systems so that they operate without him having to show up physically.

The sun rises every morning and sets in the evening.

The seed has in itself power to reproduce after its kind. This ensures continuity of everything. Systems established for wealth ensures continuous prosperity.

Genesis 8:22
While the earth remaineth, seedtime and harvest, cold and heat, summer and winter, day and night shall not cease.

Ecclesiastes 1:4-7
Generations come and generations go,
    but the earth remains forever.
 The sun rises and the sun sets,
    and hurries back to where it rises.
 The wind blows to the south
    and turns to the north;
round and round it goes,
    ever returning on its course.
All streams flow into the sea,
    yet the sea is never full.
To the place the streams come from,
    there they return again.

It's God's favour that brings money but wisdom sustains the money received.

Exodus 12:36

The LORD had made the Egyptians friendly toward the people of Israel, and they gave them whatever they asked for. In this way they carried away the wealth of the Egyptians when they left Egypt.

Proverbs 24:3-4

Through wisdom a house is built,
And by understanding it is established;
By knowledge the rooms are filled
With all precious and pleasant riches.

Poverty on the other hand is different from lack. Poverty is lack of money and knowledge that brings productivity.
Lack means no money to meet the need per time. David knew in the journey of life, needs will arise therefore he made the lord his shepherd. The lord is ever full of supply from his kingdom.

Psalms 23:1-2

The Lord is my shepherd, I lack nothing.
   He makes me lie down in green pastures,
he leads me beside quiet waters.

Philippians 4:19

But my God shall supply all your needs according to his riches in glory by Christ Jesus.

CHAPTER TWO: CAUSES OF POVERTY

1: Ignorance or incomplete knowledge of God's financial system.
When you ask believers what are the ways of God to prosper, some will say it's favor, others hard work, some will say tithing etc. There are many systems of advantage that God has set for his children. However, most believers only major in some and are ignorant of others.

Hosea 4:6
  My people are destroyed from lack of knowledge.

"Because you have rejected knowledge,

I also reject you as my priests;
Because you have ignored the law of your God,
I also will ignore your children.

Psalms 82:5-7
The 'gods' know nothing, they understand nothing.
They walk about in darkness;
all the foundations of the earth are shaken.
"I said, 'You are "gods";
you are all sons of the Most High.'
But you will die like mere mortals;
you will fall like every other ruler."

Jesus wept in two cases; one when Lazarus died and the other when he saw the ignorance of the jews.

John 11:32-35
Then when Mary was come where Jesus was, and saw him, she fell down at his feet, saying unto him, Lord, if thou hadst been here, my brother had not died.
When Jesus therefore saw her weeping, and the Jews also weeping which came with her, he groaned in the spirit, and was troubled.
 And said, where have ye laid him? They said unto him, Lord, come and see.

Jesus wept.

Luke 19:41-44
And when he was come near, he beheld the city, and **wept over it,**
Saying, If thou hadst known, even thou, at least in this thy day, the things which belong unto thy peace! but now they are hid from thine eyes.
For the days shall come upon thee, that thine enemies shall cast a trench about thee, and compass thee round, and keep thee in on every side,
And shall lay thee even with the ground, and thy children within thee; and they shall not leave in thee one stone upon another; because **thou knewest not the time of thy visitation.**

It's time to get the whole counsel of God's systems of prosperity if you want to break free from this captivity called poverty.

Acts 20:27
For I have not shunned to declare unto you **all the counsel of God.**

2: ABSENCE OF VALUE THAT IS NEEDED AND USEFUL

Value is what you offer to the world to honour the law of exchange ie, you offer value and receive money as a reward.

Many people have valuable skills and products but they are not relevant to the people around them.

You must have something the world needs.

Pay attention to the problems around you and solve them.

The master in the parable of talents found one worker to be of no value to him but the others proved valuable for they multiplied what he gave them.

Nobody will give you their money for free, you must offer value in exchange for it.

Matthew 25:14-30

For the kingdom of heaven is like a man travelling to a far country, who called his own servants and delivered his goods to them. And to one he gave five talents, to another two, and to another one, to each according to his own ability; and immediately he went on a journey. Then he who had received the five talents went and traded with them, and made another five talents. And likewise he who had received two gained two more also. But he who had received one went and dug in the ground, and hid his lord's money. After a long time the lord of those servants came and settled accounts with them. "So he who had received five talents came and brought five other talents, saying, 'Lord, you delivered to me five talents; look, I have gained five more talents besides them.' His lord said to him, 'Well done, good and faithful servant; you were faithful over a few things, I will make you ruler over many things. Enter into the joy of your lord.' He also who had received two talents came and said, 'Lord, you delivered to me two talents; look, I have gained two more talents besides them.' His lord said to him, 'Well done, good and faithful servant; you have been faithful over a few things, I will make you ruler over many things. Enter into the joy of your lord.'

"Then he who had received the one talent came and said, 'Lord, I knew you to be a hard man, reaping where you have not sown, and gathering where you have not scattered seed. And I was afraid, and went and hid your talent in the ground. Look, there you have what is yours.'

"But his lord answered and said to him, '*You wicked and lazy servant*, you knew that I reap where I have not sown, and gather where I have not scattered seed. So you ought to have deposited my money with the bankers, and at my

coming I would have received back my own with interest. So take the talent from him, and give it to him who has ten talents.

'For to everyone who has, more will be given, and he will have abundance; but from him who does not have, even what he has will be taken away. And cast the unprofitable servant into the outer darkness. There will be weeping and gnashing of teeth.'

3: LACK OF PRODUCTIVITY AND EXCELLENCE

You must have the ability to translate your value into products and services, package them with excellence and serve them to the targeted group of people.

Daniel served in all the governments during his time. It didn't matter which king was ruling. He served with excellence that all kings put a demand on his value.

He knew how valuable what he offered was that he couldn't lower his standards for anybody.

Know what you have and package it so well that many will put a demand on it. The more the people who value what you offer the more the money you will receive.

Daniel 5:12
Forasmuch as an excellent spirit, and knowledge, and understanding, interpretation of dreams, and shewing of hard sentences, and dissolving of doubts, were found in the same Daniel, whom the king named Belteshazzar: now let Daniel be called, and he will shew the interpretation.

So Daniel was brought before the king, and the king said to him, "Are you Daniel, one of the exiles my father the king brought from Judah? **I have heard that the spirit of the gods is in you and that you have insight, intelligence and outstanding wisdom.** The wise men and enchanters were brought before me to read this writing and tell me what it means, but they could not explain it. **Now I have heard that you are able to give interpretations and to solve difficult problems.** If you can read this writing and tell me what it means, you will be clothed in purple and have a gold chain placed around your neck, and you will be made the third highest ruler in the kingdom."

Then Daniel answered the king, "You may keep your gifts for yourself and give your rewards to someone else. Nevertheless, I will read the writing for the king and tell him what it means.

Daniel 6:3
King James Version
Then this Daniel was preferred above the presidents and princes, because an excellent spirit was in him; and the king thought to set him over the whole realm.

Unbelievers are more competent than believers. Believers may have spiritual advantages but unbelievers have a working mind.

Luke 16:8
And the lord commended the unjust steward, because he had done wisely; for the children of this

world are in their generation wiser than the children of light.

God allowed Moses to grow in Egypt in the house of pharaoh to get the best education so that he could write some of the books we read in the bible today.

Acts 7:22
So Moses was educated in all the wisdom and culture of the Egyptians, and he was a man of power in words and deeds.

Exodus 17:14
Then the Lord said to Moses, "Write this on a scroll as something to be remembered and make sure that Joshua hears it, because I will completely blot out the name of Amalek from under heaven."

The same with Paul, he was well educated for his purpose and needed his excellent mind.

Acts 22:3
I am verily a man which am a Jew, born in Tarsus, a city in Cilicia, yet brought up in this city at the feet of Gamaliel, and taught according to the perfect manner of the law of the fathers, and was zealous toward God, as ye all are this day.

Ephesians 3:4-5

by which, when you read, you may understand my knowledge in the mystery of Christ), which in other ages was not made known to the sons of men, as it has now been revealed by the Spirit to His holy apostles and prophets.

4: ABSENCE OF STRATEGIC RELATIONSHIPS

Religion makes you think that in life, all you need is God. However, even God when he became a man needed people to fulfil his purpose on earth.

God needed Mary to give birth to his son. Jesus needed John the Baptist to baptize him and announce him to the people.

Luke 1:26-38

Six months after Elizabeth had become pregnant, God sent the angel Gabriel to Nazareth, a city in Galilee. The angel went to a virgin promised in marriage to a descendant of David named Joseph. The virgin's name was Mary.

When the angel entered her home, he greeted her and said, "You are favored by the Lord! The Lord is with you."

She was startled by what the angel said and tried to figure out what this greeting meant.

The angel told her,
"Don't be afraid, Mary. You have found favor with God.
You will become pregnant, give birth to a son, and name him Jesus.
He will be a great man
and will be called the Son of the Most High.
The Lord God will give him
the throne of his ancestor David.
Your son will be king of Jacob's people forever, and his kingdom will never end."
Mary asked the angel, "How can this be? I'm a virgin."
The angel answered her, "The Holy Spirit will come to you, and the power of the Most High will overshadow you. Therefore, the holy child developing inside you will be called the Son of God.
"Elizabeth, your relative, is six months pregnant with a son in her old age. People said she couldn't have a child. But nothing is impossible for God."
Mary answered, "I am the Lord's servant. Let everything you've said happen to me."

Then the angel left her.

Matthew 3:13-17

Then Jesus came from Galilee to the Jordan to be baptised by John. But John tried to deter him, saying, "I need to be baptised by you, and do you come to me?"
Jesus replied, "Let it be so now; it is proper for us to do this to fulfil all righteousness." Then John consented.

As soon as Jesus was baptised, he went up out of the water. At that moment heaven was opened, and he saw the Spirit of God descending like a dove and alighting on him. And a voice from heaven said, "This is my Son, whom I love; with him I am well pleased."

John 1:29-34

The next day John saw Jesus coming toward him and said, "Look, the Lamb of God, who takes away the sin of the world! This is the one I meant when I said, 'A man who comes after me has surpassed me because he was before me.' I myself did not know him, but the reason I came baptizing with water was that he might be revealed to Israel."

Then John gave this testimony: "I saw the Spirit come down from heaven as a dove and remain on him. And I myself did not know him, but the one who sent me to baptize with water told me, 'The man on whom you see the Spirit come down and remain is the one who will baptize with the Holy Spirit.' I have seen and I testify that this is God's Chosen One."

All blessings come from God through people to you.
What you are asking God for someone has it. God grants you favor with your destiny helpers so that they can release that which you are asking God for.
Money is not in heaven, it's in people's pockets.
You need people to be prosperous.

James 1:17
Every good and perfect gift is from above, coming down from the Father of the heavenly lights, who does not change like shifting shadows.

Proverbs 21:2
The king's heart is in the hand of the Lord, as the rivers of water: he turneth it whithersoever he will.

Jesus met a man who had experienced delay only because he lacked someone to help him.

John 5:1-8

Some time later, Jesus went up to Jerusalem for one of the Jewish festivals. Now there is in Jerusalem near the Sheep Gate a pool, which in Aramaic is called Bethesda and which is surrounded by five covered colonnades. Here a great number of disabled people used to lie—the blind, the lame, the paralyzed. One who was there had been an invalid for thirty-eight years. When Jesus saw him lying there and learned that he had been in this condition for a long time, he asked him, "Do you want to get well?"

"Sir," the invalid replied, "I have no one to help me into the pool when the water is stirred. While I am trying to get in, someone else goes down ahead of me."

Then Jesus said to him, "Get up! Pick up your mat and walk." At once the man was cured; he picked up his mat and walked.

Another man had people who were willing to remove the roof to get to Jesus and he got healed.

Luke 5:17-26

On one of the days while Jesus was teaching, some proud religious law-keepers and teachers of the Law were sitting by Him. They had come from every town in the countries of Galilee and Judea and from

Jerusalem. The power of the Lord was there to heal them. **Some men took a man who was not able to move his body to Jesus. He was carried on a bed. They looked for a way to take the man into the house where Jesus was. But they could not find a way to take him in because of so many people. They made a hole in the roof over where Jesus stood. Then they let the bed with the sick man on it down before Jesus. When Jesus saw their faith, He said to the man, "Friend, your sins are forgiven."**

The teachers of the Law and the proud religious law-keepers thought to themselves, "Who is this Man Who speaks as if He is God? Who can forgive sins but God only?" Jesus knew what they were thinking. He said to them, "Why do you think this way in your hearts? Which is easier to say, 'Your sins are forgiven,' or, 'Get up and walk'?

"So that you may know the Son of Man has the right and the power on earth to forgive sins," He said to the man who could not move his body, "I say to you, get up. Take your bed and go to your home." At once the sick man got up in front of them. He took his bed and went to his home thanking God. All those who were there were surprised and gave thanks to God, saying, "We have seen very special things today."

If you desire friends, the bible says you must be friendly. You must be willing to invest time in your relationships.

Proverbs 18:24
A man who has friends must himself be friendly, But there is a friend who sticks closer than a brother.

Some people cannot be removed out of your life, God can only give you peace with them.

Proverbs 16:17
When a man's ways please the Lord, He makes even his enemies to be at peace with him.

Esther was an ordinary lady, it took his uncle to bring her to the palace where she met the king who made her queen.

Esther 2:7-8
Mordecai had a cousin named Hadassah, whom he had brought up because she had neither father nor mother. This young woman, who was also known as Esther, had a lovely figure and was beautiful.

Mordecai had taken her as his own daughter when her father and mother died.
When the king's order and edict had been proclaimed, many young women were brought to the citadel of Susa and put under the care of Hegai. Esther also was taken to the king's palace and entrusted to Hegai, who had charge of the harem.

Esther 2:17
And the king loved Esther above all the women, and she obtained grace and favour in his sight more than all the virgins; so that he set the royal crown upon her head, and made her queen instead of Vashti.

Joseph was in prison, it was a man who mentioned him to the king and he was made a prime minister of Egypt.

Genesis 41:9-14
Then the chief cupbearer said to Pharaoh, "Today I am reminded of my shortcomings. Pharaoh was once angry with his servants, and he imprisoned me and the chief baker in the house of the captain of the guard. Each of us had a dream the same night, and each dream had a meaning of its own. Now a young Hebrew was there with us, a servant of the captain

of the guard. We told him our dreams, and he interpreted them for us, giving each man the interpretation of his dream. And things turned out exactly as he interpreted them to us: I was restored to my position, and the other man was impaled."
So Pharaoh sent for Joseph, and he was quickly brought from the dungeon. When he had shaved and changed his clothes, he came before Pharaoh.

Genesis 41:37-44
Joseph's suggestions were well received by Pharaoh and his officials. So Pharaoh asked his officials, "Can we find anyone else like this man so obviously filled with the spirit of God?" Then Pharaoh said to Joseph, "Since God has revealed the meaning of the dreams to you, clearly no one else is as intelligent or wise as you are. You will be in charge of my court, and all my people will take orders from you. Only I, sitting on my throne, will have a rank higher than yours."
Pharaoh said to Joseph, "I hereby put you in charge of the entire land of Egypt." Then Pharaoh removed his signet ring from his hand and placed it on Joseph's finger. He dressed him in fine linen clothing and hung a gold chain around his neck. Then he had Joseph ride in the chariot reserved for his second-in-command. And wherever Joseph

went, the command was shouted, "Kneel down!" So Pharaoh put Joseph in charge of all Egypt. And Pharaoh said to him, "I am Pharaoh, but no one will lift a hand or foot in the entire land of Egypt without your approval."

David was a shepherd, a man mentioned him to king Saul and he was brought to serve the king.

1st samuel 16:14-23
The Spirit of the Lord had left Saul, and an evil spirit from the Lord was terrifying him. "It's an evil spirit from God that's frightening you," Saul's officials told him. "Your Majesty, let us go and look for someone who is good at playing the harp. He can play for you whenever the evil spirit from God bothers you, and you'll feel better."
"All right," Saul answered. "Find me someone who is good at playing the harp and bring him here."
 "A man named Jesse who lives in Bethlehem has a son who can play the harp," one official said. "He's a brave warrior, he's good-looking, he can speak well, and the Lord is with him."
Saul sent a message to Jesse: "Tell your son David to leave your sheep and come here to me."

Jesse loaded a donkey with bread and a goatskin full of wine, then he told David to take the donkey and a young goat to Saul. David went to Saul and started working for him. Saul liked him so much that he put David in charge of carrying his weapons. Not long after this, Saul sent another message to Jesse: "I really like David. Please let him stay with me."

 Whenever the evil spirit from God bothered Saul, David would play his harp. Saul would relax and feel better, and the evil spirit would go away.

Jesus, despite him being God, was helped by a man to carry the cross.

Luke 23:26
As the soldiers led him away, they seized Simon from Cyrene, who was on his way in from the country, and put the cross on him and made him carry it behind Jesus.

In your relationship with God, invest in it. Give time to the word, prayers etc.
Time is not found, it is created. Therefore you have no excuse as to why you cannot invest in your relationships.

Hebrews 11:6
And without faith it is impossible to please God,
because anyone who comes to him must believe that
he exists and that he rewards those who earnestly
seek him

Isaiah 45:19
"I have not spoken in secret, In a corner of a land of
darkness; I did not say to the descendants of Jacob,
'Seek Me in vain [with no benefit for yourselves].'
I, the Lord, speak righteousness [the truth—
trustworthy, a straightforward correlation between
deeds and words], Declaring things that are upright.
What or who you spend your time with is what you
value.

Matthew 6:21
For where your treasure is, there your heart will be
also.

5: LACK OF SPIRITUAL EMPOWERMENT
It's God who gives power to get wealth. This
blessing of God makes people rich. The holy spirit
teaches believers how to make profit.
On top of your skills and products that you are
offering to the world, add God's divine power and
you will overtake.

Deuteronomy 8:18
But remember the Lord your God, for it is he who gives you the ability to produce wealth, and so confirms his covenant, which he swore to your ancestors, as it is today.

Proverbs 10:22
The blessing of the Lord makes one rich,
And He adds no sorrow with it.

Zechariah 4:6
So he said to me, "This is the word of the Lord to Zerubbabel: 'Not by might nor by power, but by my Spirit,' says the Lord Almighty.

Isaiah 48:17
This is what the Lord, your Redeemer, the Holy One of Israel says, "I am the Lord your God, who teaches you to profit (benefit), Who leads you in the way that you should go.

6: IMPATIENCE
We live in a world where money has been exalted as a god and all people want to do is get rich quickly.

Proverbs 13:11
Wealth from get-rich-quick schemes quickly
disappears; wealth from hard work grows over time.

Matthew 6:24
No one can serve two masters. Either you will hate
the one and love the other, or you will be devoted to
the one and despise the other. You cannot serve
both God and money.

2nd Timothy 3:1-5
But mark this: There will be terrible times in the last
days.People will be lovers of themselves, lovers of
money, boastful, proud, abusive, disobedient to
their parents, ungrateful, unholy, without love,
unforgiving, slanderous, without self-control, brutal,
not lovers of the good, treacherous, rash, conceited,
lovers of pleasure rather than lovers of God—
having a form of godliness but denying its power.
Have nothing to do with such people.

There is a law of process for those who walk with
God. During the journey to wealth with God,
believers get the wisdom of sustaining it.

The prodigal son got the inheritance so quickly without developing capacity, he ended up losing all of it in a short time. He became worse than he was when in his fathers house.

Luke 15:11-24

Jesus continued: "There was a man who had two sons. The younger one said to his father, 'Father, give me my share of the estate.' So he divided his property between them.

"Not long after that, **the younger son got together all he had, set off for a distant country and there squandered his wealth in wild living. After he had spent everything,** *there was a severe famine in that whole country, and he began to be in need.* So he went and hired himself out to a citizen of that country, who sent him to his fields to feed pigs. He longed to fill his stomach with the pods that the pigs were eating, but no one gave him anything.

"When he came to his senses, he said, 'How many of my father's hired servants have food to spare, and here I am starving to death! I will set out and go back to my father and say to him: Father, I have sinned against heaven and against you. I am no longer worthy to be called your son; make me like one of your hired servants.' So he got up and went to his father.

"But while he was still a long way off, his father saw him and was filled with compassion for him; he ran to his son, threw his arms around him and kissed him.

"The son said to him, 'Father, I have sinned against heaven and against you. I am no longer worthy to be called your son.'

"But the father said to his servants, 'Quick! Bring the best robe and put it on him. Put a ring on his finger and sandals on his feet. Bring the fattened calf and kill it. Let's have a feast and celebrate. For this son of mine was dead and is alive again; he was lost and is found.' So they began to celebrate.

His friends who loved him only when he had money had forsaken him.

Proverbs 17:77
A friend loves at all times, And a brother is born for adversity.

Ecclesiastes 5:11
When someone's prosperity increases, those who consume it also increase; so what does its owner gain, except that he gets to see it with his eyes?

The second inheritance he got, I know he had gained wisdom on how to multiply it and spend it with the right people.

Ecclesiastes 7:11
Wisdom is good with an inheritance,
And profitable to those who see the sun.

God is all powerful but he does things in his perfect time.

Ecclesiastes 3:11
He has made everything beautiful in its time. He has also set eternity in the human heart; yet no one can fathom what God has done from beginning to end.

Jesus was in the womb of Mary for nine months, he was born in the right time of God and he grew like other children. The fact that he was God didn't make him overlook the law of process.

Galatians 4:4
 But when [in God's plan] the proper time had fully come, God sent His Son, born of a woman, born under the [regulations of the] Law.

Luke 2:52

And Jesus grew in wisdom and stature, and in favor with God and man.

7: LAZINESS
The fact that God has given believers systems of advantages like favour, anointing etc is not an excuse for laziness.
Lazy people leave all things to God not knowing there is a part for them to perform.
We are asked to imitate those who through faith and patience obtained the inheritance.

Hebrews 6:12
that ye be not lazy, but imitators of them who through faith and patience inherit the promises.

Romans 2:1
Therefore you have no excuse, whoever you are, passing judgment; for when you judge someone else, you are passing judgment against yourself; since you who are judging do the same things he does.

When God doesn't fall for their laziness, they end up stealing, being corrupt and even join Satan to get wealth quickly.

Mark 8:36
What good is it for someone to gain the whole world, yet forfeit their soul?

Luke 4:5-8
And the devil, taking him up into an high mountain, shewed unto him all the kingdoms of the world in a moment of time.
 And the devil said unto him, All this power will I give thee, and the glory of them: for that is delivered unto me; and to whomsoever I will I give it.

If you worship me, it will all be yours."
Jesus answered, "It is written: 'Worship the Lord your God and serve him only.'

God's way of getting wealth demands diligence and hard work.

Proverbs 22:29
Do you see a man who excels in his work?
He will stand before kings;

He will not stand before unknown men.

CHAPTER TWO: KEYS TO USE TO GET OUT OF POVERTY

1: A heart for God
When you set your heart fully on God, he makes you prosper. Then, he teaches you his ways so that you use money to serve his purposes in your generation.

2nd chronicles 26:5
He sought God during the days of Zechariah, who instructed him in the fear of God. As long as he sought the Lord, God gave him success.

Isaiah 2:3
And many people shall come and say, Come, let us go up to the mountain of the Lord, to the house of thc God of Jacob, that He may teach us His ways and that we may walk in His paths. For out of Zion shall go forth the law and instruction, and the word of the Lord from Jerusalem.

Psalms 35:27

Let those who favor my righteous cause and have
pleasure in my uprightness shout for joy and be glad
and say continually, Let the Lord be magnified,
Who takes pleasure in the prosperity of His servant.

2: MENTAL TRANSFORMATION
God by his power he brings money to his children
but it takes a sound mind to sustain the wealth.

Proverbs 11:16
A gracious woman retaineth honour: and strong
men retain riches.

2nd Timothy 1:7
For God hath not given us the spirit of fear; but of
power, and of love, and of a sound mind.

The mind should be educated with the word of God
so that it can think like God.

Romans 12:2
 Do not conform to the pattern of this world, but be
transformed by the renewing of your mind. Then
you will be able to test and approve what God's will
is—his good, pleasing and perfect will.

Philippians 2:5

Let this mind be in you, which was also in Christ Jesus.

Proverbs 23:7
For as he thinketh in his heart(mind), so is he.

God is not a waster, he loves increase.
Yesterday's excellence is today's mediocrity. The people who were hungry When they ate they left the bread but Jesus asked his disciples to collect what was left. He had a different mindset.

John 6:1-13
Sometime after this, Jesus crossed to the far shore of the Sea of Galilee (that is, the Sea of Tiberias) and a great crowd of people followed him because they saw the signs he had performed by healing the sick. Then Jesus went up on a mountainside and sat down with his disciples. The Jewish Passover Festival was near.
When Jesus looked up and saw a great crowd coming toward him, he said to Philip, "Where shall we buy bread for these people to eat?" He asked this only to test him, for he already had in mind what he was going to do.

Philip answered him, "It would take more than half a year's wages to buy enough bread for each one to have a bite!"

Another of his disciples, Andrew, Simon Peter's brother, spoke up, "Here is a boy with five small barley loaves and two small fish, but how far will they go among so many?"

Jesus said, "Have the people sit down." There was plenty of grass in that place, and they sat down (about five thousand men were there).Jesus then took the loaves, gave thanks, and distributed to those who were seated as much as they wanted. He did the same with the fish.

When they had all had enough to eat, he said to his disciples, "Gather the pieces that are left over. Let nothing be wasted." So they gathered them and filled twelve baskets with the pieces of the five barley loaves left over by those who had eaten.

Spiritual strength is not an excuse for ignorance.

Proverbs 23:23
Buy the truth, and sell it not; also wisdom, and instruction, and understanding.

3: PRODUCTIVITY

Package your value in products and services and serve them with excellence targeting the people that need it.

After prayers, work on how to increase your values. The higher the value you offer, the more money you will receive. The more people you offer your value to, the more money you receive.

Don't rest until you offer value to kings. Kings can reward better than common people.

Isaiah 60:3
Nations will come to your light, and kings to the brightness of your rising.

4: ABILITY TO PROVIDE SUPERNATURAL SOLUTIONS

The money you get is a report card of the problems you are solving.

There are problems all around, start providing solutions.

Exodus 31:1-6
Then the Lord said to Moses, "See, I have chosen Bezalel son of Uri, the son of Hur, of the tribe of Judah, and I have filled him with the Spirit of God, with wisdom, with understanding, with knowledge

and with all kinds of skills— to make artistic designs for work in gold, silver and bronze, to cut and set stones, to work in wood, and to engage in all kinds of crafts. Moreover, I have appointed Oholiab son of Ahisamak, of the tribe of Dan, to help him. Also I have given ability to all the skilled workers to make everything I have commanded you.

Most marriages end in divorce because of Finances. Other factors like weaknesses of partners and external factors may contribute but lack of money has been discovered to be a major contributor. Couples can pray in tongues for three hours then Satan brings an argument on money.

2nd Corinthians 2:11
in order that Satan might not outwit us. For we are not unaware of his schemes.

Many blame the spirit of poverty but it's their ignorance that strengthens it.
They are called familiar spirits for they are aware of your uncovered areas and they fashion weapons upon them.

Isaiah 54:17

No weapon formed against you shall prosper.

Weaknesses like pride, ignorance, wastage, greed
will make you a victim of Satan's schemes.
Walk with the holy spirit who will help you depend
on the Lord's grace to turn your weaknesses into
strength.

2nd Corinthians 12:9
And He said to me, "My grace is sufficient for you,
for my strength is made perfect in weakness."

Galatians 5:16-26
My counsel is this: Live freely, animated and
motivated by God's Spirit. Then you won't feed the
compulsions of selfishness. For there is a root of
sinful self-interest in us that is at odds with a free
spirit, just as the free spirit is incompatible with
selfishness. These two ways of life are contrary to
each other, so that you cannot live at times one way
and at times another way according to how you feel
on any given day. Why don't you choose to be led
by the Spirit and so escape the erratic compulsions
of a law-dominated existence?
 It is obvious what kind of life develops out of
trying to get your own way all the time: repetitive,
loveless, cheap sex; a stinking accumulation of

mental and emotional garbage; frenzied and joyless grabs for happiness; trinket gods; magic-show religion; paranoid loneliness; cutthroat competition; all-consuming-yet-never-satisfied wants; a brutal temper; an impotence to love or be loved; divided homes and divided lives; small-minded and lopsided pursuits; the vicious habit of depersonalizing everyone into a rival; uncontrolled and uncontrollable addictions; ugly parodies of community. I could go on.

This isn't the first time I have warned you, you know. If you use your freedom this way, you will not inherit God's kingdom.

But what happens when we live God's way? He brings gifts into our lives, much the same way that fruit appears in an orchard—things like affection for others, exuberance about life, serenity. We develop willingness to stick with things, a sense of compassion in the heart, and a conviction that a basic holiness permeates things and people. We find ourselves involved in loyal commitments, not needing to force our way in life, able to marshal and direct our energies wisely.

Legalism is helpless in bringing this about; it only gets in the way. Among those who belong to Christ, everything connected with getting our own way and

mindlessly responding to what everyone else calls
necessities is killed off for good—crucified.
Since this is the kind of life we have chosen, the life
of the Spirit, let us make sure that we do not just
hold it as an idea in our heads or a sentiment in our
hearts, but work out its implications in every detail
of our lives. That means we will not compare
ourselves with each other as if one of us were better
and another worse. We have far more interesting
things to do with our lives. Each of us is an original.

JOHN 13:17
NOW THAT YOU KNOW THESE THINGS,
YOU WILL BE BLESSED IF YOU DO THEM.

More Grace on you as you get out of poverty into
financial freedom.

If you need help to study God's word, email me at
pstmaryjoy@gmail.com and I will guide you
through.

To get my other books in amazon, click this link
https://www.amazon.com/author/marynyandia

www.ingramcontent.com/pod-product-compliance
Lightning Source LLC
Chambersburg PA
CBHW071121220526
45467CB00004B/1987